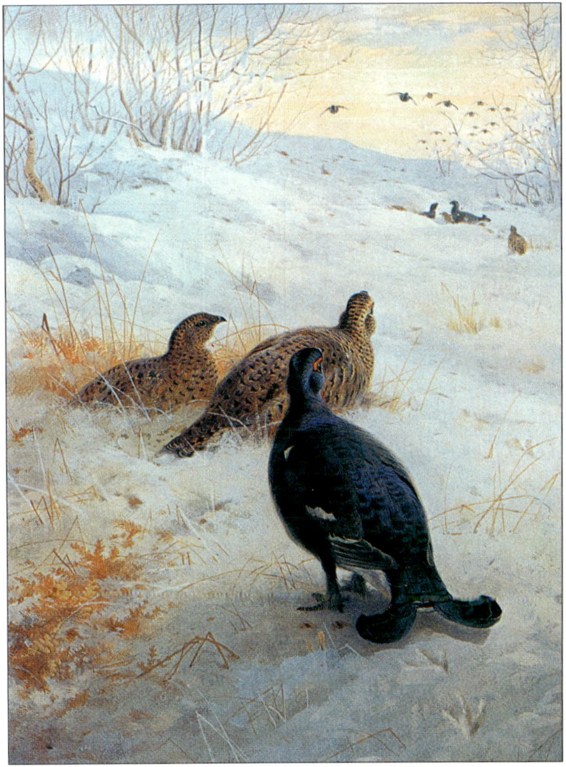

GAME RECIPES

See! from the brake
 the whirring pheasant springs,
And mounts exulting
 on triumphant wings:
Alexander Pope

with illustrations by
Archibald Thorburn

SALMON

Index

Boiled Pigeon & Bacon   18
Braised Pheasant with Whisky   13
Cotswold Rabbit Pie   15
Creamed Pheasant Casserole   22
Devilled Game   14
Exmoor Casserole   42
Fried Guinea Fowl   23
Game Stew   47
Game Pie   38
Grouse Casserole   26
Grouse Pudding   32
Irish Roast Rabbit   39
Jugged Hare   7
Mustard Rabbit   11
Partridge Pot   21
Pheasant & Apple Stew   45

Pheasant, Chestnut & Orange Casserole   35
Pheasant Soup   29
Pigeon Pudding   43
Poacher's Soup   10
Quail Casserole with Grapes   30
Rabbit & Apple Stew   34
Rich Venison Casserole   5
Roast Grouse   8
Roast Pheasant   31
Roast Partridge   40
Sautéed Pigeon Breasts   6
Venison & Chestnut Casserole   19
Venison Collops   37
Venison Patties   46
Venison Pie   24
Wild Duck with Apples   16
Woodpigeon with Mushrooms   27

Cover pictures *front:* By the Day's Bag by John Emms
back: The Young Gamekeeper by James Hardy jnr.
Title page: Blackgame Packing

Printed and published by Dorrigo, Manchester, England © Copyright

ALL KINDS OF GAME make very good eating, and pheasant, partridge, grouse, quail, woodpigeon, wild duck, rabbit and of course venison are all readily available; hares may be more difficult to come by. The initial preparation and hanging is all important and game birds need to be hung undrawn by the neck, in a cool place and protected from flies. The length of time for hanging depends on the type of game, the weather, the age of the birds and, of course, personal preference. **PHEASANT:** The most popular game bird. At their best from November to January. Young birds are excellent roasted but older birds are best casseroled. **PARTRIDGE:** Best in October. The grey English partridge is better flavoured than the red-legged or French bird, though it is smaller. **GROUSE:** August to mid-October is the best season for grouse. Hang for about one week in warm weather. Young birds can be roasted, one half bird per person, but older birds are better casseroled. **WOODPIGEON:** Pigeons are best cooked fresh; hanging is not desirable. The birds are fiddly to pluck so it is often easier just to use the breast. **WILD DUCK:** Strictly speaking wild fowl are not classified as game, but most species of duck are good to eat. **RABBIT:** The rabbit is ubiquitous as a source of meat and animals are at their best between 3 and 4 months old when they are plump and tender. Older rabbits should be stewed in some form or other. **VENISON:** Properly, only red deer meat is venison but the term is now usually used to include most other species. Venison lacks natural fat and must be kept moist during cooking. **HARE:** Hares cannot be offered for sale between 1st March and 31st July. **QUAIL:** Quail are sold ready prepared and trussed.

Voice of the Forest

Rich Venison Casserole

The gamey flavour of the meat is complemented by the rich, piquant and creamy sauce.

**2 lb. venison, cut into 1 inch cubes   2 tablespoons cooking oil or dripping
4 oz. smoked bacon, diced   1 large onion, peeled and roughly diced
1 oz. flour   1½ pints beef stock   5 fl.oz. port wine   8 oz. cranberries
8 oz. chestnuts, whole or roughly chopped (tinned or fresh)
4 oz. small button mushrooms   1 bay leaf   Salt and pepper
3 fl.oz. double cream**

Set oven to 275°F or Mark 1. If using fresh chestnuts, split the skins with a knife and cook in boiling water for about 5 minutes; then, while still warm, remove the outer skins and inner membranes. Heat the oil or dripping in a flameproof casserole dish and brown the venison cubes. Add the bacon and onion and cook for 3 to 4 minutes. Stir in the flour and cook for 1 minute, then pour in the stock and port wine and add the cranberries, chestnuts, mushrooms and bay leaf. Season to taste. Bring slowly to simmering point, cover and cook in the oven for 2 to 2½ hours or until the meat is tender. Remove from the oven, stir in the cream and serve. Serve with creamy mashed potato. Serves 4 to 6.

Sautéed Pigeon Breasts

Cooked with celery, this dish is simple to prepare and is a favourite with rough shooters.

8 pigeon breasts
2 oz. butter
1 large glass of white wine
1 medium onion, peeled and chopped

1 garlic clove, finely chopped
2 sticks celery, chopped
Salt and pepper
2 sprigs tarragon

Melt the butter in a frying pan and sauté the pigeon breasts until golden brown on both sides. Add the wine, onion, garlic and chopped celery. Season, cover the pan and simmer for 20 minutes. Then add the tarragon and continue to simmer, uncovered, for a further 15 minutes. Serve with creamy mashed potatoes and peas. Serves 4.

Jugged Hare

The name comes from the lidded stoneware jug in which this dish was originally cooked. A normal casserole dish with a lid will do equally well.

1 hare, prepared and cut into joints   Seasoned flour   1½ oz. butter
1 tablespoon cooking oil   1 onion peeled and studded with cloves
1 carrot, sliced   1 stick of celery, sliced
1 small orange, wiped and quartered   A bouquet garni
Pinch each of ground mace and nutmeg   4 peppercorns
1 pint beef stock   2 tablespoons redcurrant jelly
4 fl.oz. port wine   Salt and pepper   Butter and flour for thickening

Set oven to 350°F or Mark 4. Toss the hare joints in seasoned flour. Melt the butter with the oil in a large frying pan and brown the joints quickly all over. Remove from the pan and put into a large casserole dish with the onion, carrot, celery, orange, *bouquet garni* and spices. Pour over the stock, bring to the boil, cover tightly and simmer for about 3 hours. When the meat is tender, transfer to a serving dish and keep hot. To thicken the gravy, melt 2 oz of butter in a pan and stir in 1½ oz of flour. Add the strained liquid from the casserole and bring to the boil, stirring, until thickened. Stir in the redcurrant jelly and port and re-heat but do not boil. Pour the thickened gravy over the meat in the dish. Serve with forcemeat balls and croûtons together with jacket potatoes and a green vegetable. Serves 4 to 6.

Roast Grouse

The best way to cook a succulent young grouse is to roast it.

Brace of young grouse, plucked and drawn (retain the giblets)
2 oz. butter   2 tablespoons redcurrant jelly
Salt and pepper   6 rashers streaky bacon, de-rinded
2 slices white bread, crusts removed
Watercress to garnish

Set oven to 400°F or Mark 6. Rub a little of the butter into the well-washed and dried inside of each bird and spoon the redcurrant jelly into the cavities. Season the outside of the grouse. Cover the breasts with bacon rashers. Place the birds in a roasting tin and cover with kitchen foil. Roast in the oven, allowing 15 minutes per pound weight of one of the birds plus an additional 15 minutes. Meanwhile toast the bread. Put the giblets in a saucepan, cover with water and simmer until tender. Strain and reserve the stock to make the gravy. Remove the livers, mash them with butter, salt and pepper and spread on the toast. Slip the toast under each bird for the last 15 minutes of roasting and remove the foil. When cooked, place the grouse and the toast on a serving dish and garnish with watercress. Serve with game chips, redcurrant or rowan jelly and bread sauce. Serves 4.

The Gathering Storm

Poacher's Soup

A lovely, rich country soup which uses the left-overs from any kind of game;
pheasant, partridge, rabbit, hare etc.

Carcasses of cooked game	**1 stick celery, chopped**
Scraps of cooked game meat	**1 bay leaf**
1 tablespoon bacon fat or oil	**Sprig of fresh thyme**
2 medium carrots, roughly chopped	**8 peppercorns**
2 large onions, roughly chopped	**3 pints vegetable stock**
1 small turnip, roughly chopped	**1-2 tablespoons sherry**

2 fl.oz. double cream for serving

First heat the fat or oil in a large saucepan. Add the vegetables, cover and cook gently for 5 minutes, taking care not to let them brown. Remove from the heat. Add the broken up carcasses, the herbs and peppercorns and the stock, but reserve a little stock for blending. Bring to the boil, cover and simmer for 2 to 3 hours until the stock is really well flavoured. Strain and return to the saucepan. In a blender or food processor, purée the scraps of meat with a little of the reserved stock until smooth. Return to the pan with any remaining stock. Season and bring to the boil so that the meat is well heated through. Stir in the sherry (amount according to preference) and serve with a swirl of double cream in each bowl. Serves 6.

Mustard Rabbit

Rabbit meat and pork casseroled with a rich and creamy mustard sauce.

**1 young rabbit, cleaned and jointed   Seasoned flour (with mustard powder, salt & pepper)
A little cooking oil   ½ lb. belly pork, skinned, boned and cubed
2 carrots, sliced   1 large onion, chopped   1 tablespoon chopped fresh parsley
2 teaspoons chopped fresh thyme   1 bay leaf   Salt and black pepper
½ pint dry cider   Chicken stock   3 egg yolks   A good ¼ pint double cream
1 level tablespoon dry mustard powder   Chopped fresh parsley for garnish**

Set oven to 350°F or Mark 4. Coat the rabbit pieces with seasoned flour. Heat the oil in a large pan and lightly fry the rabbit joints. Place half the pork and half the vegetables in a casserole dish and place the rabbit joints on top. Add the herbs and seasoning and top with the remaining pork and vegetables. Pour the cider into the pan and bring to the boil. Pour into the casserole with sufficient hot stock just to cover. Cover and cook for 1½ to 2 hours until tender. Remove the meat and vegetables to a warm serving dish and keep hot. Strain the liquid into a pan and boil hard to reduce. Beat together the egg yolks, cream and mustard powder, add 3 to 4 tablespoons of the reduced liquid and whisk. Pour into the remainder of the liquid and heat through thoroughly, but do not boil or the sauce will curdle. Adjust the seasoning, adding more mustard if necessary, then spoon over the rabbit. Serve garnished with parsley, with creamed potatoes and a green vegetable. Serves 4 to 6.

The First Touch of Winter

Braised Pheasant with Whisky

The whisky adds a Scottish flavour to this dish.

Brace of pheasants, jointed
8 rashers streaky bacon
8 fresh bay leaves
3 fl.oz. vegetable oil
8 oz. shallots, peeled and left whole
6 fl.oz. whisky
10 fl.oz. chicken stock
A bouquet garni
Salt and pepper

Joint each pheasant into 4 pieces (the butcher can do this, if required). Wrap each joint with a bacon rasher, secure with a cocktail stick and tuck 1 bay leaf under the bacon. Heat the oil in a large heavy bottom pan and fry the pheasant joints until brown on both sides. Remove the joints and keep warm. Add the shallots to the pan and gently cook until softened, turning so that they are sautéed all over. Remove and set aside. Add the whisky and then the stock to the pan, bring to the boil and boil for 5 minutes, stirring continuously. Add the *bouquet garni* and season well. Return the pheasant joints and the shallots to the pan, reduce the heat and simmer gently for 45 minutes. Remove the cocktail sticks before serving. Serves 4 to 6.

Devilled Game

A quick and easy recipe to give game a delicious flavour.

4 joints of game birds (or poultry)

PASTE
4 oz. butter, softened
2 tablespoons mango chutney
1 tablespoon Worcestershire sauce
1 tablespoon Dijon mustard
1 teaspoon curry powder (to choice)
2 drops Tabasco sauce

Preheat the grill to a moderate heat. Make the paste by mixing all the ingredients together into a buttery paste. With a very sharp knife, make slashes in the skin and flesh of the game joints. Spread the paste generously over the joints and work into the flesh. Put the joints on the grill pan and grill for about 10 to 15 minutes on each side, basting with the sauce that drips into the pan. Finally, test with a skewer to ensure the meat is cooked through. Serve with the sauce poured over the joints. Serves 4.

Cotswold Rabbit Pie

This is a version of a very ancient "Poachers Pie" which has a topping of bread slices.

1 rabbit, jointed   Seasoned flour   1 oz. dripping
1 large onion, peeled and thickly sliced
2 carrots, sliced   1½ pints beef stock
Salt and black pepper
4 oz. mushrooms, wiped and thickly sliced
3 large slices white bread (crusts on), thickly cut; about ½ inch or more
Chopped fresh parsley to garnish

Set oven to 350°F or Mark 4. Dust the rabbit joints with seasoned flour. Melt the dripping in a large pan and fry the joints all over to brown. Add the onion and carrots, pour over the stock, season to taste and bring to the boil. Transfer the whole to a casserole dish, cover and cook for 1 to 1½ hours until the rabbit joints are tender. Add the mushrooms. Cut the bread slices in half diagonally and dip one side into the gravy.   Place on top of the casserole mixture, gravy side up, and cook in the oven for a further 40 minutes, uncovered, until the bread has become crisp.   Serve sprinkled with chopped parsley and accompanied by boiled potatoes. Serves 4.

Wild Duck with Apples

*Wild duck have a distinctive but not a fishy flavour, as is sometimes thought.
If preferred, a domestic bird can be used instead for the recipe.*

**2 wild ducks or 1 duck approx. 5 lbs, prepared
3 oz. butter   1 tablespoon oil   3 tablespoons brandy
¼ pint white wine   ½ pint chicken stock   Juice of ½ orange   Salt and pepper**

**APPLE SAUCE
1 lb. cooking apples, peeled, cored and sliced
4 tablespoons cider or water   2-3 tablespoons sugar   2 oz. butter   Pinch of cinnamon**

Set oven to 325ºF or Mark 3. Wipe the bird(s) inside and out and rub the skin with salt and freshly ground pepper. Heat the butter and oil in a large flameproof casserole and brown the duck(s) all over. Warm the brandy, pour over the duck(s) and set aflame. Next, pour over the wine and stock, bring to the boil, cover and cook in the oven for 1½ to 2 hours. When cooked, transfer the duck(s) to a serving dish and keep hot. Meanwhile, strain the cooking juices into a bowl, spoon off the fat and return to the casserole. Add the apple sauce and orange juice, heat through and stir well. Pour over the duck(s) and serve with boiled potatoes and a green vegetable. Serves 4. **Apple sauce.** Simmer the apples in a saucepan with the cider or water until soft, add the sugar and butter and cinnamon and beat well.

Tenants of the Lake

Boiled Pigeon and Bacon

As pigeons are fiddly to pluck, it is best just to use the breasts.

4-6 pigeon breasts   4 oz. bacon scraps
1 medium onion peeled and studded with cloves
1 stick celery, roughly chopped   2 carrots, roughly sliced
A bouquet garni   Salt and pepper
¾ pint vegetable or chicken stock
Butter and flour for thickening

First fry the bacon scraps in their own fat, adding a little oil if necessary. Transfer to a large saucepan and fry the pigeon breasts in the bacon fat until well browned. Add to the bacon in the pan with the onion, celery, carrot and *bouquet garni*. Season with salt and pepper and pour over the stock. Bring to the boil, cover and simmer for 1 to 1½ hours until the meat is tender. Transfer the pigeon and bacon to a serving dish, arrange neatly and keep hot. Remove the *bouquet garni*. To thicken the gravy melt 2 oz butter in a pan and stir in 1½ oz flour. Add the strained liquid from the pan and bring to the boil, stirring. Pour the thickened gravy over the meat in the dish and garnish with fried mushrooms. Serve with boiled potatoes and spinach. Serves 4.

Venison and Chestnut Casserole

A rich, gamy casserole which is cooked slowly for a long time and needs to be started the night before.

**3 lbs. venison, cut into 1 inch cubes
1 pint stout   ½ pint red wine
1 bay leaf   1 teaspoon juniper berries, crushed   1 sprig thyme
1 small onion, peeled and finely chopped
3 tablespoons cooking oil   1 tablespoon flour   Salt and pepper
12 oz. tinned whole chestnuts**

Place the cubed venison, stout, wine and herbs in a bowl, cover and leave overnight to marinate. Next day set oven to 275°F or Mark 1. Remove the meat from the marinade, drain well and dry with kitchen paper, reserving the liquid with the herbs. Heat the oil in a flameproof casserole and add the meat, a few pieces at a time, to brown. Remove the meat from the casserole and add the onion. Cook for a few minutes until lightly browned. Return the meat to the casserole, stir in the flour and cook gently for 1 minute. Gradually add the marinade liquid with the herbs, stirring all the time. Season to taste with salt and pepper. When the mixture boils, cover, place in the oven and cook for 2 to 3 hours until the meat is tender. Add the chestnuts for the last 10 to 15 minutes of cooking time, to heat through. Serves 6 to 8.

September Siesta

Partridge Pot

For years the English or grey partridge has been in decline but today, with careful management, it is making a comeback. This is a good recipe for older birds.

Brace of partridge, cleaned and jointed   Seasoned flour
2 oz. butter   1 small onion, peeled and chopped
1 clove of garlic, peeled and crushed   ½ lb. button mushrooms, wiped
4 tomatoes, skinned and halved   4 slices lean ham, chopped
Pinch dried thyme   4 cloves   6 peppercorns   Salt   Pinch of sugar
1 glass port wine   1 to 1½ pints chicken stock   A little cornflour

Dust the partridge joints with seasoned flour. Melt the butter in a large saucepan and brown the joints lightly on all sides. Add the onion, garlic, mushrooms, tomatoes, ham, thyme, spices, salt and sugar to the pan. Combine the port with the stock and pour over. Bring to the boil, then cover and simmer very slowly for 2 hours or until the partridge joints are tender. Remove the joints to a warm serving dish, dredge out the vegetables with a slotted spoon and arrange round the joints. Keep hot. Discard the cloves and peppercorns and skim the remaining liquid. Blend the cornflour with a little cold water and add to the gravy. Bring to the boil, stirring, until the gravy has thickened a little, then pour over the partridge joints and the vegetables. Serve the stew accompanied by triangles of hot toast. Serves 4.

Creamed Pheasant Casserole

Birds of an uncertain age or from frozen storage can be converted into this tender meal.

**A brace of pheasants, prepared   2 sticks celery, sliced
1 carrot, sliced   1 onion, sliced   1 bay leaf   Salt and black pepper**

**SAUCE: 2 large onions, chopped   Oil for frying   2 oz flour   8 fl.oz. crème fraiche
4 tablespoons mango chutney   2 tablespoons Worcestershire sauce
1 tablespoon mushroom ketchup   1 small tin peaches in juice
1 tablespoon chopped fresh parsley**

Trim the pheasants, put into a large pan with the stock ingredients and cover with water. Bring to the boil then simmer for 1½ to 2 hours until the pheasants are very tender. Leave to cool in the liquid. When cool, strip the meat from the bones and skin, cut into neat pieces and reserve. Strain the stock. Heat the oil in a large pan and fry the onions until soft but not browned. Add the flour, stir in 8 fl.oz of the reserved stock and bring to the boil stirring, to thicken. Remove from the heat and stir in the crème fraiche, chutney and sauces. Stir in the pheasant meat and, if the sauce is too thick, thin down with a little more stock. Transfer to an ovenproof dish. Drain the peaches very well and cut into cubes. Before serving, stir half the peach cubes into the sauce mixture and reheat for about 20 to 30 minutes until bubbling hot. Garnish with the remaining peaches and chopped parsley and serve. Serves 6 to 8.

Fried Guinea Fowl

*Originally a game bird, guinea fowl are now farmed as poultry.
They are in best condition between February and June.*

**1 large guinea fowl, about 3 lb, cleaned and jointed   Seasoned flour
2 oz. butter   1 large onion, peeled and finely chopped or minced
3 oz. streaky bacon, chopped   4 oz. button mushrooms, wiped
¼ pint dry white wine   Salt and black pepper   Watercress to garnish**

Joint the guinea fowl, place in a saucepan and cover with water. Bring to the boil, cover and simmer for about 1 hour, skimming once or twice. Remove the joints from the pan, strain the stock and boil the liquid hard to reduce to about a ¼ pint. Meanwhile, dust the joints with seasoned flour. Melt the butter in a frying pan and gently fry the joints until lightly browned. Remove and keep hot. Put the onion in the pan and fry until soft and transparent, adding more butter if necessary, then add the bacon and fry, stirring, until lightly crisp. Add the mushrooms and fry, stirring, for a further minute. Pour in the wine and the reduced stock and bring to the boil, stirring. Return the guinea fowl joints to the pan, cover and simmer for 5 minutes, seasoning to taste. Remove the joints and place on a warmed serving dish. Spoon the sauce over them, and serve garnished with watercress. Serves 3 to 4.

Venison Pie

The combination of venison, red wine and redcurrant jelly makes a delicious rich pie.

**2 lb. venison shoulder, cut into 1 inch cubes   2 oz. flour
Pinch ground mace   Pinch of all-spice   Salt and pepper
5 fl.oz red wine   5 fl.oz. red wine vinegar
10 fl.oz. venison or beef stock   2 onions, peeled and sliced
½ tablespoon chopped fresh parsley
1 tablespoon redcurrant jelly
12 oz. puff pastry**

Set oven to 450°F or Mark 8. First tenderise the meat with a mallet or rolling pin and remove any fat or gristle. Mix the flour with the mace and all-spice and season well with salt and pepper. Dust the cubed meat with the flour mixture. Put in a saucepan with the wine, vinegar and sufficient stock to cover the meat. Cover and simmer gently for 1 hour, then add the onions and parsley. Simmer for another 30 minutes. Remove from the heat, allow to cool and skim off any fat from the surface. Put the meat mixture in a pie dish, add the redcurrant jelly and the remaining stock. Roll out the pastry on a floured surface, cover the pie, seal the edges, make a steam hole and bake for about 25 minutes until the pastry is golden brown. Serves 4 to 6.

The Monarch of the Glen

Grouse Casserole

This is a good way of cooking slightly older grouse, with the added flavour of whisky.

Brace of grouse, trussed **1 stick of celery, chopped**
3 oz. butter **2 carrots, diced**
1 onion, chopped **2 tablespoons whisky**
4 oz. mushrooms, chopped **10 fl.oz. chicken stock**
1 tablespoon redcurrant jelly

Set oven to 350°F or Mark 4. Melt the butter in a heavy casserole dish and brown the grouse all over. Remove from the casserole and set aside. Add the chopped and diced vegetables to the casserole and cook gently until soft but not browned. Return the grouse to the casserole. Warm the whisky, pour over the grouse and set aflame. When the flames have disappeared add the stock. Bring to the boil, cover and simmer for about 1¼ hours. When cooked, remove the grouse and, using shears, cut each bird in half, set aside on a large serving dish and keep hot. Strain the liquid into a saucepan and boil fast to reduce. Reserve the strained vegetables. When the gravy starts to thicken add the redcurrant jelly, allow it to dissolve and then spoon over the grouse with the strained vegetables. Serves 4.

Woodpigeon with Mushrooms

Woodpigeons have for long been shot by farmers as an ongoing pest.
Although taking some time to cook, their slightly gamy flavour makes a tasty casserole.

4 woodpigeons, prepared   2 oz. butter   2 tablespoons oil
2 medium onions, sliced   8 oz. mushrooms, halved
1 large cooking apple, peeled, cored and sliced
2 tablespoons cranberry jelly
1 bay leaf   ¼ pint chicken stock   1 cup cider
1 heaped dessertspoon cornflour
Salt and pepper

Heat the butter and oil in a large, flameproof casserole and brown the birds all over. Remove and set aside. Lower the heat and fry the onions, until lightly browned. Remove from the heat and add the mushrooms, apple slices, cranberry jelly and bay leaf and season well. Place the pigeons on the mixture and pour over the stock and cider. Bring to the boil, cover and simmer for 2 to 2½ hours, stirring occasionally. When the pigeons are tender, remove and set aside. Remove the bay leaf. Drain off the liquid into a pan and stir in the cornflour, already mixed with a little water. Bring to the boil, stirring until the liquid thickens. Return the gravy to the casserole with the pigeons, stir well and finally heat through gently. Serves 4.

Watched from Afar

Pheasant Soup

A clear soup; just the thing for a dinner party. Not as expensive as it sounds.

1 pheasant, cleaned and jointed
1 large onion, peeled and roughly chopped
2 carrots, sliced   1 leek, sliced   2 sticks celery, chopped
A bouquet garni   1 blade of mace   12 peppercorns   Salt
2 teaspoons lemon juice   4 tablespoons port wine or sherry
1 stick celery, finely diced and blanched

Put the pheasant joints, onion, carrots, leek, celery, herbs, mace and peppercorns in a large saucepan. Add salt to taste and one teaspoonful of the lemon juice. Add sufficient cold water to cover. Bring to the boil, then cover and simmer over a very gentle heat for 4 hours. Strain well, reserving the best pieces of pheasant meat. Allow to get cold, then skim off all the surface fat and remove the *bouquet garni*. Dice the reserved meat. Pour the soup into a saucepan, add the diced pheasant meat and bring to the boil. Stir in the port or sherry. Serve the soup garnished with the finely diced celery, which has been blanched in boiling water to which 1 teaspoon of lemon juice has been added. Serve with fingers of hot toast. Serves 4.

Quail Casserole

Quail are uncommon in the wild, but are reared on game farms and sold ready prepared for the pot. Allow two birds per person for a main course. Quail need no hanging.

4 quails, prepared and trussed   Salt and pepper
4 vine leaves (if available)   4 rashers streaky bacon, de-rinded
1 oz. butter   4 oz. green grapes, peeled and de-seeded
4 tablespoons game or chicken stock
2 tablespoons brandy

Set oven to 400°F or Mark 6. Rub the birds with salt and pepper and wrap each one first with a vine leaf (if available) to bring out the flavour, and then with a rasher of bacon. Melt the butter in a pan and sauté the birds for 10 minutes to brown all over. Transfer the birds to a heat-proof casserole dish and arrange the grapes around them. Pour over the juice from the pan and cook in the oven, uncovered, for 5 minutes. Add the stock and brandy, cover the dish and cook for a further 5 minutes or until the birds are tender. Serve with mashed potatoes and a green vegetable. Serves 2.

Roast Pheasant

The rich sauce complements the game flavour of the pheasant.

1 large pheasant, prepared   3 rashers streaky bacon   2 oz. butter, melted
1 tablespoon redcurrant jelly   5 fl.oz. white wine   Juice of ½ lemon   4 slices white bread

STUFFING
8 oz. pork sausagemeat   1 small onion, finely chopped
1 dessert apple, peeled, cored and finely chopped
2 tablespoons chopped fresh parsley   Salt and pepper   1 egg, beaten

Set oven to 350°F or Mark 4. First make the stuffing. In a bowl, mix together the sausagemeat, onion, apple, parsley and seasoning and bind with sufficient of the beaten egg. Stuff the pheasant (any stuffing left over can be shaped into balls and cooked round the bird). Place the pheasant in a roasting tin and wrap the bacon rashers round the bird. Brush all over with the butter and roast for about 35 to 40 minutes. Remove from the oven and drain off the fat. Pour the wine over the pheasant with the redcurrant jelly and lemon juice. Return to the oven for about another 20 to 25 minutes, basting frequently. Meanwhile, fry 4 slices of bread. When the pheasant is cooked and the juices run clear when a skewer is inserted, remove from the oven and cut into quarters. Place the pieces on the fried bread on warm plates and keep warm. Transfer the roasting tin to the heat to boil and reduce the sauce. Pour over the pheasant to serve. Serves 4.

Grouse Pudding

A steamed suet pudding made with a mixture of grouse meat and rump steak.

**1 grouse   ½-¾ lb. rump steak   Seasoned flour
1 onion, peeled and finely chopped   Salt and pepper
1-2 tablespoons Madeira or port wine   ½ pint chicken stock
18 oz. suet pastry**

Grease a 2 pint pudding basin. First make the suet pastry. In a bowl, mix 12 oz self-raising flour and 6 oz shredded suet with just sufficient cold water to make a stiff paste. Roll out on a lightly floured surface and use two-thirds to line the pudding basin. Strip the meat from the grouse and chop with the beef into small pieces. Coat the meat in seasoned flour. Fill the lined basin with the mixed meats and the onion and season. Add the wine and sufficient stock to cover the meat. Cover with the remaining pastry and seal the edge. Cover the basin with greaseproof paper and cover and seal with kitchen foil. Steam for about 4 hours, adding more stock through a hole in the crust after 2 hours. Serve with mashed potatoes and a green vegetable. Serves 4.

Covey of red Grouse

Rabbit and Apple Stew

A simple way to convert rabbit joints into a tasty meal.

4-6 joints of rabbit   Seasoned flour   2 oz. butter
2 medium onions, chopped   2 medium carrots, sliced
2 medium apples, peeled, cored and thickly sliced
8 oz. mushrooms, sliced
8 oz. streaky bacon, cut into 1 inch pieces
½ pint vegetable stock   2 teaspoons tomato purée
Sprig of fresh thyme or 1 teaspoon dried thyme
Salt and pepper

Heat half the butter in a large saucepan and cook the onions, carrots and apples for 5 minutes, stirring well. Remove from the pan and set aside. Toss the rabbit joints in the seasoned flour. Heat the remaining butter in the pan and brown the rabbit joints on both sides. Lower the heat, add the mushrooms and bacon pieces and continue cooking for 5 minutes. Add the stock slowly and then add the reserved apple/vegetable mixture, the tomato purée and thyme, stirring all the time, and season. Bring to the boil, cover, lower the heat and simmer for 1 hour or until the rabbit is tender. Stir occasionally and add more stock or boiling water if required. Serves 4 to 6.

Pheasant, Chestnut & Orange

A brace of pheasant, prepared   Oil for frying
6 oz. whole chestnuts (tinned or fresh)
2 oz. flour   ½ pint red wine   1 pint chicken stock
2 medium onions, peeled and thickly sliced
Rind and juice of 1 orange
1 dessertspoon redcurrant jelly
Salt and black pepper

Set oven to 275°F or Mark 1. If using fresh chestnuts, split the skins with a knife and cook in boiling water for about 5 minutes; then, while still warm, remove the outer skins and inner membranes. Heat a tablespoon of oil in a large frying pan and brown the pheasants all over. Transfer to a large casserole dish. Put the chestnuts in the pan, brown all over and add to the casserole. Add another tablespoon of oil to the pan, stir in the flour and cook gently for 1 minute. Stir in the wine and stock and boil until thickened slightly. Add the onions, orange rind and juice and cranberry jelly to the pan and season well. Pour the contents of the pan into the casserole dish with the pheasants and chestnuts, bring to the boil, cover and cook in the oven for 3 to 4 hours until the pheasants are tender. Check the seasoning, remove the orange rind and serve. Serves 6 to 8.

The lost Stag

Venison Collops

Steaks cut from the haunch or loin chops are equally suitable for this dish.

**8 venison steaks (6 oz each)
Salt   Black pepper   Cayenne pepper   Ground nutmeg
Oil for frying
¾ pint red wine   Juice of ½ lemon   1 pint venison or beef stock
1 oz. butter   1 oz. flour**

First season the steaks with salt, pepper, cayenne and nutmeg. Heat sufficient oil in a pan and fry the steaks quickly to seal and brown the meat. Then lower the heat and continue frying for about 15 minutes or until tender. When cooked, transfer to a serving dish and keep warm. Add the wine, lemon juice and stock to the pan and bring to the boil. Knead together the butter and flour into a ball, add to the gravy and continue boiling to thicken. Adjust the seasoning and pour over the steaks. Serve with mashed potatoes and a green vegetable. Serves 8.

Game Pie

Pheasant or partridge with steak and bacon form the basis of this substantial pie.

**1 pheasant or a brace of partridge, cleaned and jointed
8 oz. stewing steak, cut into 1 inch cubes
Seasoned flour   2 rashers streaky bacon, cut into strips   1 oz. butter
1 onion, peeled and chopped   A little seasoned flour   1 oz. button mushrooms, wiped
A bouquet garni   Salt and black pepper   1 pint prepared brown stock
10 oz. shortcrust pastry or flaky pastry   1 beaten egg**

Set oven to 300°F or Mark 2. Melt the butter in a pan and fry the onion until just soft; remove and set aside. Dust the steak with seasoned flour, brown lightly in the pan and place in the bottom of a deep pie dish. Repeat with the pheasant or partridge joints, place them on top of the meat, then scatter over the reserved onion, the bacon strips and mushrooms. Add the herbs and season to taste. Pour on sufficient stock to cover, cover with kitchen foil and cook for 1½ to 2 hours. Remove from the oven and allow to cool. Increase oven to 400°F or Mark 6. Remove the herbs and discard, then add sufficient stock to bring the level to about ½ inch from the top of the filling. Roll out the pastry on a floured surface, cover the pie and trim. Decorate and brush with beaten egg. Bake for 20 minutes, then reduce oven to 300°F or Mark 2 and bake for a further 15 minutes or until the pie is golden. Serves 4 to 6.

Irish Roast Rabbit

Being Irish, this rabbit is not roasted at all, but is casseroled in milk in the oven!

1 rabbit, jointed   Vinegar and water mixed
2 tablespoons flour   ½ teaspoon dry mustard   Salt and black pepper
2 oz. butter   2 onions, peeled and chopped   4 rashers bacon, de-rinded and chopped
1 dessertspoon chopped fresh parsley   ½ teaspoon chopped fresh thyme
½ pint milk

Soak the rabbit joints in the vinegar and water for about 30 minutes. Drain and pat dry on kitchen paper. Set oven to 375°F or Mark 4. Mix the flour, mustard and seasoning together and coat the rabbit joints. Melt the butter in a frying pan and lightly brown the rabbit joints on both sides. Place in an ovenproof casserole. Fry the onion in the remainder of the butter until soft, then add to the casserole with the bacon and herbs. Heat the milk until just below boiling point and pour over. Cover and cook for 1 hour or until the rabbit is tender. Serve with boiled potatoes, carrots and a green vegetable and accompanied, if desired, with parsley sauce. Serves 4.

Roast Partridge

*Partridge are at their best in October and roasting is ideal for a young bird.
It should be hung for 4 days or more according to weather and taste.*

1 partridge, cleaned and trussed
A lump of butter worked up with salt and pepper and lemon juice
A vine leaf (if available)
1 or 2 rashers of fat streaky bacon
Croûtons of fried bread
Lemon slices and watercress to garnish

Set oven to 400°F or Mark 6. Insert the lump of seasoned butter inside the partridge and place the bird in a well-buttered roasting tin. If available, tie a vine leaf over the bird to bring out the flavour, and lay over the bacon rashers. Roast for about 20 minutes and serve on a bed of croûtons of fried bread. Pour over the pan juices and garnish with slices of lemon and with watercress. Serve with game chips and a green vegetable. Serves 1 to 2.

Hard Times

Exmoor Casserole

Venison is low in fat and therefore cooking it as a casserole is an excellent, moist method of preparation. This dish has a better flavour if made the day before it is required and then re-heated.

2 lb. venison, cut into 1 inch cubes   2 tablespoons cooking oil
2 oz. butter   2 medium onions, peeled and diced
2 cloves garlic, crushed   2 tablespoons flour
1 pint beef stock   ¼ pint port wine
8 oz. black cherries, stoned (if using tinned cherries, drain well)
1 bay leaf   Salt and black pepper

Set oven to 350°F or Mark 4. Heat the oil and butter in a frying pan and fry the venison cubes, a few at a time, until well browned all over, and transfer to a large casserole dish. Add the onions and garlic to the pan and cook gently until soft. Stir in the flour and cook for 2 to 3 minutes. Add the stock and port wine stirring all the time, and bring to the boil. Stir in the cherries, add the bay leaf and seasoning and pour the mixture over the meat in the casserole dish. Cover and cook in the oven for 1½ to 2 hours until the meat is tender. Remove the bay leaf and serve hot with mashed potatoes and green vegetables. Serves 4 to 6.

Pigeon Pudding

Pigeon breasts and stewing steak combined within a suet crust.

**Breasts from 3 pigeons   ½ lb. stewing steak   Seasoned flour
1 onion, peeled and sliced   Good pinch dried mixed herbs
Chicken stock   1 tablespoon red wine   Salt and pepper
12 oz. suet pastry**

Grease a 1½ to 2 pint pudding basin. First make the suet pastry. In a bowl, mix 8 oz self-raising flour with 4 oz shredded suet with just sufficient cold water to make a stiff paste. Roll out on a lightly floured surface and use two-thirds to line the pudding basin. Cut up the pigeon breasts and steak into neat pieces and coat in seasoned flour. Fill the lined basin with the meats, onion, herbs, 2 to 3 tablespoons stock and the red wine and season. Cover with the remaining pastry as a lid and seal the edges. Cover and seal with kitchen foil and steam for at least 4 hours, topping up the water as necessary. When the pudding is cooked and opened, add some extra hot stock. Serve with a green vegetable. Serves 3 to 4.

The Bridle Path

Pheasant and Apple Stew

Use Egremont Russet or similar apples to give the stew a spicy apple flavour.

1 pheasant, prepared
2 oz. butter
2 lb. Egremont Russet apples
1 onion, peeled and chopped
4 juniper berries
Pinch of dried thyme
1 bay leaf
1 glass of apple juice
Salt and pepper

Melt the butter in a large saucepan and sauté the pheasant until brown all over. Meanwhile, peel and core the apples and leave them whole. When the pheasants are browned, add the chopped onion, berries, herbs and seasoning, pour in the apple juice and surround the pheasant with the whole apples. Bring to the boil, cover the pan and simmer until the pheasant is tender. When cooked, remove the pheasant and apples to a serving dish and keep warm. Boil down the pan juices and thicken with a little cornflour blended with a little cold water to make the gravy. Serve with roast potatoes or game chips and a green vegetable. Serves 2.

Venison Patties

These little meat balls make a tasty dish with a piquant sauce.
They are a good way to use up left-over cooked venison.

1 lb. cooked venison meat, minced
1 small onion, very finely chopped or minced
1 thick slice white bread, crusts removed
1 egg, beaten   Salt and pepper   Butter for frying
½ pint prepared white sauce
1 tablespoon French mustard   1 teaspoon sugar
Dash of Worcestershire sauce
1 teaspoon horseradish sauce (if desired)

Set oven to 375ºF or Mark 5. Crumble the bread in a bowl with a fork, mix in the minced venison and the onion and bind with sufficient of the beaten egg. With oiled hands form the mixture into little round, flattened patties about 1 to 1½ inches in diameter. Melt the butter in a pan and fry the patties gently on both sides until browned and transfer to an ovenproof dish. Prepare ½ pint of white sauce and stir in the mustard, sugar and Worcestershire sauce. A teaspoon of horseradish sauce added will give the sauce more bite. Pour the sauce mixture over the patties and bake for 30 minutes. Serve hot with mashed potatoes and a green vegetable. Serves 4.

Game Stew

Use any variety and mixture of game meats to make this flavoursome stew.

1 lb. mixed game meat e.g. grouse, venison, hare etc.
2 oz. ham, diced   Seasoned flour
2 oz. butter   1 small onion, peeled and chopped
1 carrot, chopped   2 sticks celery, chopped
¾ pint game or beef stock   3 fl.oz. red wine
Salt and pepper

Cut the game meat into cubes and toss in the seasoned flour. Dice the ham. Melt the butter in a heavy bottom casserole dish. Fry the vegetables until soft, then add the game meat and ham and continue frying until browned. Add the stock and red wine. Bring to the boil, cover with a lid and simmer gently for 1 to 1½ hours, skimming occasionally. Season and serve with mashed potato and redcurrant or rowan jelly. Serves 4.

METRIC CONVERSIONS

The weights, measures and oven temperatures used in the preceding recipes can be easily converted to their metric equivalents. The conversions listed below are only approximate, having been rounded up or down as may be appropriate.

Weights

Avoirdupois	Metric
1 oz.	just under 30 grams
4 oz. (¼ lb.)	app. 115 grams
8 oz. (½ lb.)	app. 230 grams
1 lb.	454 grams

Liquid Measures

Imperial	Metric
1 tablespoon (liquid only)	20 millilitres
1 fl. oz.	app. 30 millilitres
1 gill (¼ pt.)	app. 145 millilitres
½ pt.	app. 285 millilitres
1 pt.	app. 570 millilitres
1 qt.	app. 1.140 litres

Oven Temperatures

	°Fahrenheit	Gas Mark	°Celsius
Slow	300	2	150
	325	3	170
Moderate	350	4	180
	375	5	190
	400	6	200
Hot	425	7	220
	450	8	230
	475	9	240

Flour as specified in these recipes refers to plain flour unless otherwise described.